FIRE SERIES / // ///

PITT POETRY SERIES

Nancy Krygowski and Jeffrey McDaniel, *Editors*

FIRE SERIES / // ///

POEMS

KELLY HOFFER

Published by the University of Pittsburgh Press, Pittsburgh, Pa., 15260

Manufactured in the United States of America
Printed on acid-free paper
10 9 8 7 6 5 4 3 2 1

ISBN 13: 978-0-8229-6768-2
ISBN 10: 0-8229-6768-5

Cover and book design by Alex Wolfe

Publisher: University of Pittsburgh Press, 7500 Thomas Blvd., 4th floor, Pittsburgh, PA 15260, United States, www.upittpress.org

EU Authorized Representative: Easy Access System Europe, Mustamäe tee 50, 10621 Tallinn, Estonia, gpsr.requests@easproject.com

slash, *n.* Felled trees and other debris left in a forest after logging or the clearing of a tract, or resulting from high wind or fire.

CONTENTS

FIRE SERIES / // ///

A field (not on fire)

a field moves
like water
grasses the sea   the sea
quieting
                                the flaming thing

God is a kite.

the tether pierces my palm. I would have given
up my hands earlier for this relief
of a bodily mark of the intangible. I have never
been a person of faith, made as I am
of stiffer stuff. salt and tits and shallows. shadow
preserves snow, each object has its own
frosted cape in the shape of its shade. I am
threaded through. I walk
among the melting ice. holding
or being held, are you a kite or am I a doll
hanging by a string. a lemon thread
between two cans—do I
bring one to my ear in search of
ocean, or do I drag them both
behind my nuptial convertible, baby blue,
hearing nothing I know

my mother is still dead, and I am still
a child.

God is a kite.

after sex I wake back to
myself, estranged from what
my body has finished
doing and the things
I didn't teach it. it was an animal
worrying a neck. he goes to wash, I
lie and recollect. the pain
in my jaw that subsided for the duration
returns and my breasts settle
into their creases, newly meat. the rushes on the side
of my mind's stream quiver into stillness.
am I, was I predator.

am I prey.

The first symptom of a sequel

late, I arrived thinking I was early.

as arriving is always being belated   to goings on already

going. every lemon I write is a note for my lover who loves

Jack Spicer.   I fail to keep

our language empty.   citrus has a season, but lately all my days

have been wearing winter, cuffing season, too,

a comfort to be chained even   with lips soured

worrying a candied peel   good luck escaping

such charms   the glowing centers of the innumerable small

blue flowers make a constellation for my memorial impulse

to draw strings across   needing branches to hold the baubles

I extend again from my torso   an offering   seeded   with potato eyes

this   year has brought many and more

losses than our grieving dovecote can bear, we are bird-poor recruiting new animals to announce the dead

obituary after obituary dissolves, skywritten smoke   I remain

dazzled even by the glint off ice, hungry for things bright of flavor

I write to   him—a missive, an arrow, a plea, a ball approaching the temperature of the sun

to stand under   the burning thing   I fold into a sheet

fitted to the curve of the earth

this is my favorite lemon

he was leaving, but I arrived

the faces of a diamond

I left her like a jilted bride

like her, I left, a jilted bride

jolly like a bride, I jilted

her her her her

like a her, I was left

hurting, jilted

joyous, I was left

I left, I felt
                    the size of it

////

//

/

The first flame named only after expulsion

Genesis 3:24

So he droue out the man: and he placed at the East of the garden of Eden, Cherubims, and a flaming sword, which turned euery way, to keepe the way of the tree of life.
—King James Version (1611)

So **He drove the man out**; and at the east of the garden of Eden He stationed the cherubim and the flaming sword which turned every direction to guard the way to the tree of life.
—New American Standard Version (1995)

So he drove out the man; and he placed at the east of the garden of Eden the Cherubim, and the flame of a sword which turned every way, **to keep the way of** the tree of life.
—American Standard Version (1901)

So he sent the man out; and at the east of **the garden** of Eden he put winged ones and a flaming sword turning every way to keep the way to the tree of life.
—Basic English Bible

And he drove out Man; and he set the Cherubim, and the f**lame** of the f**lash**ing sword, toward the east of the garden of Eden, to guard the way to the tree of life.
—Darby Bible

So he drove out the man: and he placed at the east of the garden of Eden Cherubim, and a flaming sword which turned every way, to keep the way of the tree of life.
—Webster's Bible

So he drove out the man; and he p**lace**d Cherubs at the east of the garden of Eden, and the flame of a sword which turned every way, to guard the way to the tree of life.
—World English Bible

yea, he **cast**eth **out** the man, and causeth to dwell at the east of the garden of Eden the cherubs and the flame of the sword which is turning itself round to guard the way of **the** tree of life.
—Youngs **Literal** Bible

So He drove out the man; and He placed at the **ea**s**t** of the garden of Eden the cherubim, and **the flaming** s**word** which turned every way, to keep the way to the tree of life.
—Jewish Publication Society Bible

Pluming

the mind shivers

between two forms

in the morning I am a rabbit

in the evening I am a duck the poem the line trailing

the sun, never quite catching where to? which animal

is it becoming, which mammal are you

abandoning I follow the fiery dot the horizon pens me in

night comes to me

extending its feathers

/

to end

on an image is to avoid   a decision   yet here I stand

still, in two streams, water collaring   my ankles each

prickling in its sensuous confusion   I think about the dying

I will be doing some day   sight goes

before hearing, so I am told   our last images I imagine

are sonic ones

an abstract fantasia   glows in green   and rust blooming

/

the more I write the more I find myself weaving

a tenuous line

having thought   the thought too often about

my last words to my mother

her last words to me—I worried them down, I fear

I have lost them

I fear   my poems

about her death will replace her

/

I am constant in my   remaking, making

my memory in my own image, a plaintive, soft-plated mouth (if I am a bird, I am a young one)

photographs may (I ask permission)   correct our grief, but they are always also

grieving, a death mask is the image

I do not want

to end on   when my mother died, her eyes were already

closed and she was surrounded

by the sound of her children holding their breaths

listening for her to leave the room

/

how do I protect my mother from   my lyric tendency

to add the ornament, be it poison or polish or pith

/

a poet (one who loves me) tells me that I try so hard

to make my language bloom, asks what would happen

if I asked it to do something other
than   flourish

/

what image did my final liquid message leave on the screen

of my mother's dying brain   did it move   was it beautiful

did my last sounds come to her

as fireworks come

to a child closing their eyes and tapping

out sparks   on their eyelids

///

/

//

A structured fire

returns to the bed
repeats the flame
the flame revisits the curtain
the curtain is drawn to reveal a
flame curtaining   a recursive
entity
              dancing in the window

An unstructured fire

a fire in a field   begins
almost no   fire at all   the
origin not the true
place of catching
a matchhead survives—the live-
stock escape   unless sheltered
by barn beams   this array
defining the vector blaze   a tail smoking
in the hay-flare
                              their ears burnt past eating

Ars poetica (clouded)

this morning I came to the document

in search of clarity, pining for that egress

of a cloud moving away from the

back of my neck where my extra eyes lie

looking over a glacial pool—

here, I say, it is so simple to start over.

I open another window, discard the last,

send it floating, out on the water. the pool is milky,

filled with stone ground to powder, clouded.

but I've talked, too often,

about clouds, this not my first, nor my last.

the parable, I remember, opens with a painter

whose studio went up

in flames. she lost her life's work and

was relieved. when she painted

again, she painted the paintings her

immolated paintings had only dreamt of. a canvas

of a cloud of smoke lifting

off a pool. a canvas of a flame

extinguishing. a figure in gray. my

poems linger even without

document. I've read them

to myself, in my little silence, in my quaint

ritual way that to

lose them would be to, would be predicated on,

losing my mind, to watch it float

away wrapped in a latex balloon. instead, the air is clotted

with my thoughts, persisting there

beyond my will. without poems I am not

sure I would know

the cloud

when I saw it. but I can admit

sometimes I want my brain

to burn up, hoping as I do, to

see the cloud, and write it out,

once again for the first time

without metaphor

///

///

Fire interval

three cranes, painted yellow, crest the mountain face *fire* below, the gas barbecue on the hotel deck wears a little coat for storage *fire* on the trail we talk about strip club bureaucracy and department stores and I find a flower called Prettyface *fire* a strange name for a theater, a strange name for a lion *fire* Adam calling the animals calls himself *fire* I forget my body for a minute *fire* back at the resort I watch a video of someone's hands tapping an overturned ceramic vessel to center it on a wheel for trimming *fire* the video tells me to hold my fingers at three, seven, and ten o'clock *fire* angels, keeping busy, tidy needles in heaven's corner *fire* the labor of the spinning disc *fire fire* Adam names the lodgepole pine before he has need of shelter *fire* I watch a video from above *fire* a pool I cannot sound *fire* I think *fire* not for the first time *fire* of Adam without interior *fire* Adam with no rooms to enter *fire* Adam with no rooms to offer *fire* what would he make of my face crowned in *fire fire fire* an exit without a room to feed it and who is roaring through *fire* evening'll be coming round the mountain when she comes

the faces of a diamond

she wore silk roses in her hair

she wore roses, her hair silk

she wore down the roses

with her fingers, worrying

she handled the silken case

silk becoming thread, like hair

the silk becomes her

her fingers, rosy, stripping corn

she wore cornsilk, she was roses

she rose, and said, *here*

/////

//

/

///

chemical lace / day series

morning/

the new light new again still unclear

where the rays finally go absorbed into infinite so-and-so

running stitch the cord of my legs

chain link ripples some tree flesh

a new form of execution my body has never been unsafe

unless in public due to its holes have you been laced through

like a purse, pierce a drink of tall water

noon/

a tulip without its shadow

disclosure of the full image   the sun a coin   I can't look at

divulge a turning   if a face is the part of a thing presented to view   but I cannot bear to receive

the present   the hot ray   diffused across warming skin   my tits pooling

the sun's skin radiating itself   touching even the side of the universe I haven't seen

stuck as I am on

my particular cloud

deep afternoon/

fealty singing a pearl a pronounced quantity pearling   a number of incisions down the beast

of the tone   poised on   an edge of a cliff   like my flourish? like my pith?

fluorescence   petalpetalpetal   becoming my own   little pet dusk/

the parting of the thing into   shallow and deeper dark

evening/

kept to the garden the gibbous hanging by a sacrificial thread pull thru to

the next window bobbing on the evening tide wrapping the loom

in sparkling

night is mapped with noise venus comes up to cast her even pattern

shadow of the tread alighting

chemical lace / day series

morning/

the new light new again still unclear

where the rays finally go absorbed into infinite so-and-so

running stitch the cord of my legs

chain link ripples some tree flesh

a new form of execution my body has never been unsafe

unless in public due to its holes have you been laced through

like a purse, pierce a drink of tall water

noon/

a tulip without its shadow

disclosure of the full image the sun a coin I can't look at

divulge a turning if a face is the part of a thing presented to view but I cannot bear to receive

the present the hot ray diffused across warming skin my tits pooling

the sun's skin radiating itself touching even the side of the universe I haven't seen

stuck as I am on

my particular cloud

deep a**ft**ernoon/

fealty **sing**ing a p**e**arl a **p**ron**ounce**d quantity pea**r**l**ing**   a **numb**er of incisions **down** the beast

of **the** tone   **pois**ed **on**   an edge of a cl**if**f   like my f**lou**ri**sh?** like my pith?

fluore**scen**ce   petalpe**t**alpetal   **be**com**ing** my own   **lit**tle pet dusk/

the parting of the thing into   shallow and deeper dark evening/

kept to the garden   the gibbous hanging by a   sacrificial thread   pull thru to

the next   window   bobbing on the evening   tide   wrapping the loom

in sparkling

night   is mapped with noise   venus comes up to cast her even pattern

shadow of the tread   alighting

/

/

/

//

Or am I a room with a roof taken off, still holding onto my idea of a ceiling

the other night I woke in the early morning
and texted myself, "can you hear a fire"
not asking about the moment
then but about the potential
of a moment of being proximate
to heat and feeling it with my ears.
my sleeping self, thinking not, I think, of
the domesticated crackle of our
gatherings out in the cold of what
will be remembered as the time
of collective sickness and the collective fear
of sickness approaching. the hearth kept us civil
for half an hour. my sleeping self, tentative, opening,
asks her virtual self, does a wall of fire
sound on the scale
of a waterfall? the roaring of what could be
mistaken to be a highway
filled with metal
containers moved by their combusting
innards. I realize then, we mistake water

for fire all the time, every morning after a
heavy rain when the world is especially
recalcitrant. in the case of the non-
virtual fire, temperature or smell
or of course, the glow, is what, I assume,
we render first,
but I am stuck on the sound of something
big enough to kill me.
we shave the grasses down
to a bristled penumbra, we build bonfires
from the slash to convince
ourselves of our reckoning,
newly unsettled, that this is the planet
we've mastered, we hold our invisible
ceilings without shelter
standing aside the effigies of our problems
papier-mâchéd, caricatured, features too large
as if we made the feelings big enough
they would take up
and leave, not taking up

so much space inside us.
the fire department is on call, waiting
for things to get out
of control, still,
the morning after the fire
doesn't burn me up
my snot is laced with black ribbons.
next to the flames, I did not register the smoke—
what dollhouse tragedy were we
playing at.

/////

//

/

/
///
//
///

///
/

The first flame wed to a sword

Genesis 3:24

So he droue out the man: and he placed at the East **of the garden** of Eden, Cherubims, and a flaming sword, which turned euery way, to keepe the way of the tree of life.
—King James Version (1611)

So **He drove the man out**; and at the east of the garden of Eden He stationed the cherubim and the flaming sword which turned every direction to guard the way to the tree of life.
—New American Standard Version (1995)

So he **drove out the man**; and he placed at the east of the garden of Eden the Cherubim, and the flame of a sword which turned every way, to keep the way of the tree of life.
—American Standard Version (1901)

So he **sent the man out**; and at the east of the garden of Eden he put winged ones and a flaming sword turning every way to keep the way to the tree of life.
—Basic English Bible

And he **drove out Man**; and he set the Cherubim, and the flame of the flashing sword, toward the east of the garden of Eden, to guard the way to the tree of life.
—Darby Bible

So he **drove out the man**: and he placed at the east of the garden of Eden Cherubim, and a flaming sword which turned every way, to keep the way of the tree of life.
—Webster's Bible

So he **drove out the man**; and he placed Cherubs at the east of the garden of Eden, and the flame of a sword which turned every way, to guard the way to the tree of life.
—World English Bible

yea, **he casteth** out **the man**, and causeth to dwell at the east of the garden of Eden the cherubs and the flame of the sword which is turning itself round to guard the way of the tree of life.
—Youngs Literal Bible

So He drove **out the man**; and He placed at the east of the garden of Eden the cherubim, and the flaming sword which turned every way, to keep the way to the tree of life.
—Jewish Publication Society Bible

Eve on fire // the hymn

for years I'd advocated for a horizontal transcendence

a body that wasn't mine I was ready for

I paid for what I didn't know

—a piano—

plays itself in a cavernous mall

so you have desire, what's next

there's more and then there's less

—a black streak—

across a tree

something arrived and it was too much

—something smaller—

survived the burning

the wind makes a flag of the geyser

carrying its white water across the sky

what does water stand

up for

I paid to know a body that wasn't

—mined—

come to me for what you can't take

—out of me—

the surviving thing the smaller for it

lilies rise up out of water

—where's the ground—

above their spindling reflections

he told me to *rise up* was redundant   I told him falling

was a kind of birth   and the tide was big enough for both

of us

Eve on fire // the siren

I wrote “horizontal transcendence”

but it is ecstasy

—the thing I protect from language—

the most precious outpourings nurse a jolt

spinning inward   toward a diamond

refusing duration but I keep on

being, and can’t help

—the mirror over my shoulder—

is the woman in the pane

one of the captured

the internet a giant pool and I go there to drink

the internet of its substance

I search out the lilies I found

—in a photo—

coming out of water

they require a flood to flower but are not water

—they are not water lilies—

lies the woman

in pain   and what else

would she be, only true

—like my mind—

in the named world, a figment

in the literal

two men tell me two somethings and ask me

to arbitrate but

—what is your name—

and

—where can I live—

where the medusa

is not a woman captive

in the desert   she is a cactus and

—is not a woman—

a callous budding from her side

the magenta fruit, the waxy skin pocked

an animal buckling into its habit

—is not a woman—

—is not a woman—

—and—

—here's an image—

of spindles   and fangs

the shadow of

a foot stepping on a diamond

pattern that warns

of

—is not a woman—

poison

//

//

flame

I want him

he finds

me

the thing on

fire

flame

I tell him

I want him

want

want

want

he finds

me

his I am

the thing wanting he won't

want

fire

old flame

I tell him what
I want I want him
to tell me what I
want I want what I
want to be what he
is I want to
be his wanting I am wont to
want he wouldn't he finds
me wanting I am
his if he wants if he's wanting I am
always the wanton thing wanting he won't
will to
want
he hangs fire

/ /////

/
/
/

Brood parasite

if we agree we take
possession of the things
that bear us,
if we agree
to brood is *to cherish with the mind.*
to brood is to try to hold a cloud in your mouth without letting
on that it's there. the nest doesn't belong to the hatchling as it belongs
to the eggs. if we accept a possession
is the thing you own, is the ghost that rules you.
a hatchling *takes* possession, empties a nest by pushing eggs
over the woven lip with its unfeathered tail.
property is a two-way street, I like to think.
my mother for example, my grief for another.
the broken eggs belong to the ground, and the ground
to the blood-streaked yolks—
an example, even, belongs to its abstract shell.
ownership is an obstacle to unletting,
sex better on a rented bed, pleasure freer overheard
by a faceless neighbor. the baby
didn't speak my tongue but
I understood her wanting language all the same.

a cloud is the egg you hold in your mouth,
the baby the thing you can't help
but let in. spun sugar is the cotton you consider
breathing. the egg, I cherish it with my mind.
my mind, a mouth sitting on top of a nest.
all the same, birthright is the fiction
America builds in me. meeting
my neighbors I call them siblings. singing
false, I evict them without sprouting a feather.
the joy I expected
in abetting another's abandonment
never arrives. my country, inescapable,
escapes me. the world condenses to a word,
the candy in the sky starts to cry,
my tears sustain a thing, cherishing.
a taut relation is a two-way string—
talking into the tin can,
talking into an echo, I derail its shape.
I have forgotten the egg I came from, the one
I came for. I have forgotten

if I am bigger or smaller than my mother—
the natural order, she understands my wanting
language.
my mouth opens, cherry-stained,
I am hungrier than she can stand
to provide.

In the early dark of morning

the birds made an eels' nest

with their voices, trills ribboning to silver

tails plashing in and out of

deep and deeper

liquid, the black air carrying

its frenzy to me wet and slickened

roiled I woke to the sound with

its glinting carom

                                        I knew light

was still far off

Constraints I give the page as it builds my virtual life

peach in my mouth, I want to you to suck on the fuzzy heart

any mishap should be Eros waiting in a hedge, every meeting cut with foliage

the foreground and background oscillate beyond arbitration

clouds unsettlable, they are lighter or darker or lighter than the sky

lashes fall from my eyes without ceremony

there will be a wringer for clothes, a ringer for bells

my team will be stacked with sorrow

every patch of earth nominated by a commemorative plaque

I want anger to come only in flashes and leave without residue

I want a loop of my mother cheering

too loud in a grade-school gymnasium

the dream takes flesh, clay cracks and falls from your shoulders

I want to forget the things I want

to forget

my mother calls the mountain a woman and she's out every day

your desire for me is of a size

undeniable, embarrassing

I want the drama of a snowcap

and for heat to be just

heat

Field holiday

well aren't we

special and isn't this

a good way to wind

up in a couple's costume

you the daddy and me the momless

released into a cornmaze looking for

the goatkid braying

like a human

                    I'm done

being quiet holding a braying

of my own   and it shudders

                    I've been making

light-based art very quaintly

and cooking and feeling tight

in last year's clothes   I lean into it

more tit for you and new

underwear for me   nice to be

a facet like a face of an

object for a little while

at least   I'm getting

less pretty and more toothy

I'm sorry are you   unfamiliar

with the animal version of my

jaw   dressed in an excuse

to become a different character in

the same sex fantasy where now

you're the one   to tell

me hello by taking me

into your mouth and you make

no noise

tell me if I'm blushing   am I

blushing   the color

of my nipples   flashes up

to the ears   my face lined

with a tissue   hot, endless—

look at my face

watch my mouth   get dressed

up like a trick gift and tell me

the pretty things I've done

well   and how good

it makes me

//

//

//

//

Do I *take to the heather*

like I take to

take a shine to the virtual flame and how long the curtain it makes for me

a screen bathing me in a robe of braided light

or do I take

like a waterbird to water

I am a grassbird holding a hard-kernelled heart in my beak

Do I *set the heather on fire*

like I set a table   like I set

a row of curls

          I set a field

          I set the agenda

          I, the matter to unrest

do I keep my hair in a vise   becoming outlaw

          nothing more ordinary than

a setting sun
          my vices overtake   the blazing noon, I've come too early

and at high altitudes   your shoulder rocks me toward a burnished coin

in the wind, the blade of the thicket sharpens   dresses my calves in welts

I go mowing and uncover a nest

ants spill from the amulet they've buried in the ground

the brush brushes me

into a corner   a landscape becoming a law   I realize its logic

the hallway thru the grass is ten times the thickness of my body

my affinity for property   my limit

////////////////   //////////////
////////////////////////////////
////////////////////////////////
////////////////////////////////
//////////////// ///////////////
//////////////// //////////////
//////////////// //////////////
///////////////   /////////////
////////////////////////////////
////////////////////////////////
////////////////////////////////
////////////////////////////////
////////////////////////////////
////////////////////////////////
////////////////////////////////
////////////////////////////////
////////////////////////////////
////////////////////////////////
////////////////
////////////////
//////

///

///

Disaster type

I am in the part of love where I move somewhere new and the only
thing calling me is locusts that come to eat someone else's crop—

I am in a land where I have grown nothing.

a sink hole swallows months of spring's slow work, I watch blades of grass follow one
and another, lemminglike off a vacuum's cliff.

all of God's surface is such a ledge in the making. settling down
a kind of violence, even if muffled and wet.

I am in the part of love where I begin to understand abandonment,
the doing of it—knowing well the being done.

I put "piss" in a poem and take it out like the woman
who awaits me in my old age, removing her teeth.

of what I have left behind, I hope I leave the self, its cilia and all
its precious loyalties, preciousness, as such.

sleepers or eaters, which is your plague? the buzz of fluorescence lights a new
singing sphere. still, the locusts.

I keep a miniature luxury, a thumb-sized square of silk to turn
and return to. it will grow nothing but softer.

I put my teeth back in.

He told me he recognized our new life and I knew

I carried a tick with me all day
and did not know. he sent me word

across a lake covered in a mist rising
and then forgot he had

he thought the word again
and again sent it

fashioned a boat-
shaped hole out of the same mist

curtains come together and
disappear their seam

the little woman on the stage of my heart cannot
find an exit in the velvet

I love to be picked up and then put down
put down and then picked up

I can be a doll, I can be your accent
thread pulled through a loom

if you are going to fix me
in place, let my place be your first

point of orientation, tell me
how you'd like me to fashion—

I want to know you as every pronoun, but I keep
my eyes for myself

does the stage of his heart have a little man—
does he turn his face—to the house or to the curtain?

we talk about how we need
a system for screening poison from our home

something stiffer than a talisman's
collective agency

which life, which arrow
I consign, I elect

I roll up my sleeve and see in the imprint
of the elastic cuff, a freckle walking

we have our four hands on the vane of the house
moving the weather

the mist closes, again more pliable
than velvet

the stage of my heart is an apse
and I empty to it

he calls through the velvet
checking in on the universe

now if only
he were calling
for me

the faces of a diamond

less thing than I realized

the thing I realized less

a girl lies, a thing across a bed

the less I realized, the more the thing

the lessening   alive again

/

////

/////

///////
///////
///////
///////
///////

///   //
//
/

The first flame a vehicle

Genesis 3:24

So he droue out the man: and he placed at the East of the garden of Eden, Cherubims, and a flaming sword, which turned euery way, to keepe the way of the tree of life.
—King James Version (1611)

So **He drove** the man out; and at the east of the garden of Eden He stationed the cherubim and the flaming sword which turned **every direction** to guard the way to the tree of life.
—New American Standard Version (1995)

So he drove out the man; and he placed at the east of the garden of Eden the Cherubim, and the flame of a sword which turned every way, **to keep** the way of the tree of life.
—American Standard Version (1901)

So he sent the man out; and at the east of the garden of Eden he put winged ones and a flaming sword turning every way to keep the way to the tree of life.
—Basic English Bible

And he drove out Man; and he set the Cherubim, and **the flame** of the flashing sword, toward the east of the garden of Eden, to guard the way to the tree of life.
—Darby Bible

So he drove out the man: and he placed at the east of the garden of Eden Cherubim, and a flaming sword which turned every way, to keep the way of the tree of life.
—Webster's Bible

So he drove out the man; and he placed Cherubs at the east of the garden of Eden, and **the flame** of a sword which turned every way, to guard the way to the tree of life.
—World English Bible

yea, he casteth out the man, and causeth to dwell at the east of the garden of Eden the cherubs and the flame **of the sword** which is **turning** itself round to guard the way of the tree of life.
- Youngs Literal Bible

So **He drove** out the man; and He placed at the east of the garden of Eden the cherubim, and the flaming sword which turned every way, **to keep** the way to the tree of life.
- Jewish Publication Society Bible

vers

the static

vers -e proof of a shared

a- vers -ion to the effects of turning—

vers -us *this,* the

vers -e as plow line, as plumbline, this an

ad- vers -e possession, territory unmoored from its owning/

vers -us,

happy

anni- vers -ary, once more together in an egg-shaped loop around the sun. are you well

vers -ed in my verity, I am. a lady. I am

re- vers -ing course, a girl in the shadow of the duchess—she

a- vers a statement of her truth, her diminution, her turning into a very-much-indeed

in- vers -ion of herself, yet unknown but familiar, familial,

a vision in silk, a tufted

vers -ace handbag in hand/

vers -e

con- vers -ing, a conference, a gem, a collection of

ob- vers -e

facets/

vers -atile, virile, ventral

ver~~s~~ -ging on the far-from-virginal, crested in

ver~~s~~ -million. the proclamation released with labile swiftness, a fortress denser/

vers -ed in the tinny regulation, she

disco- vers it is over, our covert dalliance. observe. a ferrous powder

co- vers the chandelier/

vers -se-beguiled, she is spelled
with a

vers -al letter. a fearsome voice exposed, virgule hanging. a tongue drips diamonds.
the ad

vers -e tuning the atmosphere hot. pink. a martian palace of

vers -ailles. the

uni- vers -e is single-mouthed, sucking its sound into a pocket. balancing on a

vers -ant slope, housed in a formal garden of my choosing, I open
my chest to the weather

Sex poem

and then God said
let there be non-being
and the non-being was
good

Pygmalion iteration

if I am a bird, I am a pigeon
if you are a bird, you are a dove

if I am a fountain, I am dyed green for a holiday
if you are a fountain, you are filled with coins

if I am a pigeon, I am molting
if you are a dove, you are pearl white,
molten, and phoenix-boned

I sit on your ledge and pull
change from your belly

if I am a woman, I am an animal, if I am not
an animal what am I
if you are an animal, you are the magpie who catches
himself in a mirror, a round yellow sticker
on your feathered throat

I am a whatnot with a beak
I am a palm with glinting teeth

if I am a voice, I am a body
if you are a voice, you are an echo of

an animal, you are an animal
if you are an animal crying

if you are a celestial object, you are a sun
burning the film of dew off a summer's lawn

if I am a face, I cry into my hands until my eyes disappear
if you are a face, you are a mouthless cliff

if I am a mollusk, I am the poison mussel, cooked and firmly shut
if you are a mollusk, you are pearl-less

if I am a celestial object, I have forgotten
if I am a pearl, I was born of sand
you are not a pearl, and I open my mouth to
forget the man of you

I try to climb you without footholds, you shift away from my hands
my face becomes an animal, crying

if I am a dune, I am shaped like a slick of ice cream
I taste sweet, I breathe salt

if you are a dune, you are shaped like a cloud

Firebreak

how do you protect a body from language,

be it poison or polish or pith?

may I? I ask permission—*dismal, downy,* resigning

my name

how do I convince him to want

my protection, my speculative   *will you*

the slash   making territory

out of fuel

a forest

riven

An exercise in which I try to see blue in the red flame.

when I write toward the world, I am pushed out of it.

fingering language's tether, I ask to be opened.

the saying about cake is a trinity: wanting—eating—having.

duality, framed as a contradiction, forgets desire.

the mouth insists, an abject shuttle.

my wanting turns on the invitation to move through, but not out:

I'm pulled back, into the fold.

if you must return to me after a long absence, let me protest first this length.

let me pick the season.

I take you to the winter woods and show you the apartment building newly visible through trees.

the branches are naked, and then, to the sky, so are we.

the pace of a miracle, something sudden.

when you say "serious as a heart attack," I think of how rapid a fall from the ledge of eye level.

I place my thoughts in rabid water.

a man suspended from the jungle gym curls his legs into his body; he remains the same height.

when I picture winter in my mind, I place an orange in a neat bed of snow.

I am so busy in my ritual gesture, I forget to be simultaneous.

the metaphor delights, the lake swallows, the noise drowns.

as if a landscape drapes a body in paint.

as if the gilded frame.

heat, colorless, rises from the vent in my neighbor's rooftop, shimmering the air.

I suggest we reconsider the past or I imagine you handling it as I have—shaved of a protective awning.

the grid, a fine mesh, objects to my movement and rewards me with a mirage.

my ears prickle in the cold—any exterior burns me.

leaving its forks lying on the table, the future makes for an exit.

the weather is either coming or going.

fulfilling its own bidding, a season undoes itself.

driving into the night's forehead, I see snow suspended: an explosion of tails.

the thing I desire, the cause of my suffering.

my desire, too, causes me suffering.

if I must countenance it, why not be its object.

cake with a thick slather of icing.

doing a puzzle, I piece together little men.

my hand is a spotlight on the line, I follow its thread into a void, seeing before me never more

than a breath's length.

you become the orange.

I call it again, a slice at a time.

my tongue lets me make of you a hymn.

I know language is plenty alive because when he calls me a good girl, I come.

////

///

//////////////

Racket (i)

law-abiding with an itch

for undoing

contrition

practicing clauses

in my sleep as to how to

be the most active, the least

passive, as to how to be such

as anything like

a vector

/

eligible, legible I

saying the what of

my want and the giving

what for to what I un-

want, heaving

am I one of the unserious

my impatience has come

unquiet

/

the rage in my little pretty

head arranged against

the ordering principle

scale, embarrassing

limbs intact, a docile rage, really

every violence

in my experience

theoretical except

what my money does

in its free time, what

cost

/

to be abstract, useful

allowance, an opportune

shiver in the concept

am I, aren't we

how does it feel

to be included

ear an eraser to be

had in the head

in the hand a mirror

and what good

timing

/

looking for a light

that escapes politeness

offering to be un-

pleasing—

create a mark

-et?

no, thanks

be the boss of any

thing except

my own sentence

read that

any way you want

/

don’t just

stand there

help

refusal get up

off the

ground

Racket (ii)

on a kick with repetition

tricked out in

new plumes of smoke

on a continent just

forming hard edges

in the mind—

hello, windfall, hello

toxic uptick

is this the good fruit, she asks,

is this the good labor?

the money on the grid

is a new brand of color

mirage-bright

cone-worthy

an object

I am overly

it

/

an ethic of making

one’s own luck stuck

fingering shine

trailing ribbons

call me a prize pig!

suck on a line

entertaining a denial

tone, how’s your solitaire

dance-card? care to

ask where I got hitched—

the moon sputters through

its sickly honey

/

where have you gone

having spent

the good time

no one gave you

where can I go where

my language would

not follow

Racket (iii)

painted false eyes

on warships

to turn them mammal

bite here! avoid the brains

of the operation

lashes strategic in their shade

we keep the monument

in working order

/

I'd be done with

this if I didn't feel

done in by

that, that is

undone

on a loop

that, is

grains spilled on

the horizon of a

voice on a

high-wire

tight-hope

tongue-tuck

dip-trick

bad to feel all

the electric fences

of the body

(the ins and outs)

of a want

of too few

options

/

my most capable

concept

eyeless—

nimble when it comes

to things we think to kill

in the dark

/////
//
/
/

/

/

Know where

:   my ability to move through

my body with my eyes

closed   I have become a wandering   humor

she listened

              where I was breathing

grasses shift with the same   flickering static

of waves coming off an ocean,   I

              know how   to map this

facility, essence mobile   terrain baggy ripe

for pillage   it was hardest

for me   when she hesitated

to voice her   voiceable pain   pain's language is,

wretchedly, available to us

what face do we give it

what hushing gift do we drape over its mouth

in the field I can't help but return to

I turn my head to hear her diastole, the blood she is letting,

carried on her exhale,

I turn my head to greet her with my ear,

and she kisses my neck

Foliage freeze

a burr   catching brittle
engulf frame   stilted con-flag
-ration blaze blue   fervid crucible flare
sentimental white-hot pining   lick charred
elementary particles in sense   caught
a liar   vexing   consonant in heat

the heather is soft   dangerous
the earth is brushed   dangerous
an upswell of heat is not for
once about anger
this is energy moving without
me even if
I want it   to taste
my spites   nestle petty sparks

a fire holds no flag but its own   leaves
still   waving

I am a worried
husk
smoking

The first flame rendered

Genesis 3:24

So he droue out the man: and he placed at the East of the garden of Eden, Cherubims, and a flaming sword, which turned euery way, to keepe the way of the tree of life.
—King James Version (1611)

So He drove the man out; and at the east of the garden of Eden He stationed the cherubim and the flaming sword which turned every direction to guard the way to the tree of life.
—New American Standard Version (1995)

So he drove out the man; and he placed at the east of the garden of Eden the Cherubim, and the flame of a sword which turned every way, to keep the way of the tree of life.
—American Standard Version (1901)

So he sent the man out; and at the east of the garden of Eden he put winged ones and a flaming sword turning every way to keep the way to the tree of life.
—Basic English Bible

And he drove out Man; and he set the Cherubim, and the flame of the flashing sword, toward the east of the garden of Eden, to guard the way to the tree of life.
—Darby Bible

So he drove out the man: and he placed at the east of the garden of Eden Cherubim, and a flaming sword which turned every way, to keep the way of the tree of life.
—Webster's Bible

So he drove out the man; and he placed Cherub**s** at t**h**e east of the garden of Eden, and the flame of a sword which turned every way, to guard the way to the tree of life.
—World English Bible

yea, he casteth out the man, and causeth to dwell at the east of the garden of Eden the cherubs and the flame of the **s**word w**h**ic**h** is turning itself round to guard t**h**e way of t**h**e tree of life.
—Youngs Literal Bible

So He drove out the man; and He placed at the ea**s**t of the garden of Eden the c**h**erubim, and t**h**e flaming sword which **turn**ed every way**,** to **keep** the way to the tree of life.
—Jewish Publication Society Bible

///   ///////   ///   /////   //

I invest in horizon futures

I lie when I say to my desire, *I'm sorry, I didn't know*
you were waiting

my desire and I talk around a covenant
a former version of myself extracted a promise not to be

stuck in line holding someone
else's purse—I have been lying

around my apartment in a shroud aspiring
to a vision filled with constellated flares

my desire watches me undress and talks to me about anything
other than my body

what's the damage? I give and open
I pay with plastic, I pile another grain of sand on my doubt

adjusting a swimsuit along the curve of my ass, I show my desire
a glimpse of that lighter flesh

at least a line is going somewhere
to be broken

this, my "plucky" disposition—*tell me again*, that story of elegance
my jealousy is embroidered with threads so expensive

I am ashamed
of my wasting habit, I am recovering

from conjugal logic—I drape myself in an ankle-long net
of seedling pearls and call

the woman in the mirror
a bride

no one is happy, but here
is my impression

this blue recedes to reveal another
borrowed blue

I lied when I said to my
desire, *I didn't know you*

the faces of a diamond

I held real lilacs in my hands, and turned

I, a real girl, held lilacs and turned

real, the lilacs, held me

reeling, I grew a handle to be carried, really to be handled

is there anything   more like the real

than turning in   lilac hands   where I seek nothing

and sleep

NOTES

Epigraph

definition of "slash" taken from the *OED*: "slash, n.1." *OED Online*, Oxford University Press, September 2021, https://www.oed.com/view/Entry/181388

"Do I *take to the heather*"

definitions of "heather" taken from *OED*: "heather, n." *OED Online,* Oxford University Press, December 2022, https://www.oed.com/view/Entry/85177

"chemical lace/day series"

Chemical lace is a textile produced by embroidering a fine mesh and then submerging the fabric into a chemical solution to dissolve the mesh substrate. This process leaves behind a finely stitched lace design.

"Genesis" series

The various translations of Genesis 3:24 were taken from https://www.kingjamesbibleonline.org/

ACKNOWLEDGMENTS

With deep thanks to the editors of the publications where versions of these poems found their first homes:

Afternoon Visitor
American Chordata
Gulf Coast
Hobart
Hood of Bone Review
Mercury Firs
Paperbag
PDF Mag
Poetry Northwest
Post45 Contemporaries
Sixth Finch
Washington Square Review
Works & Days
Yum! Lit

//

And to Bryce with love—for sitting with me fireside.